OF MEN AND MONSTERS

POEMS AND FRAGMENTS

OF MEN AND MONSTERS

POEMS AND FRAGMENTS

Jeff Senatra

EMPTY HANDS ETC. PRESS

Copyright © 2018 by Jeff Senatra

All rights reserved

First Compilation: Lion Pose Press 1996

New Edition: Empty Hands Etc. Press 2018

Cover design and illustration by the author

POEM TITLES AND FIRST LINES

Messenger Of The Crows

Separation   1

Under The Arc   2

City   3

To Have Left   4

The Moon   5

Swift Robed   6

Porpoise Hills   7

Ghosts And Dreams   8

To Be A Slavic Warrior   9

Night/Great Inky Masked   10

Cloud   11

Full of Corridors   12

Demise Ensues Calm Order   13

Storm   14

Murky Children Along The River   15

I'm Amazed By Sight   16

Ancient   17

Prelude (News Of Departure)   18

Ghost In The Iris   19

The Carriage Lurches On   20

Small Gifts Enable Adventure   21

Drought Trails Us   22

Dog Vision   23

Ascent   24

Born Of Fire   25

In The Becoming Of The Hollow   26

Reentering The Lights Of Town   27

Of Men And Monsters

Lying Lawlessly Along The Moon's Tracks   31

Do You Know What It Is   32

Systematic   33

With Open Eye And Open Mouth   34

Meat Tooth, Time   35

Symptoms   36

To Live   38

A Call To Darkness   39

I Will Follow You   40

Return, Clash   41

Breeding Season   42

Somber Casings   43

Beauty Embraces   44

Mating Trick   45

Terror Chased Her   46

He Placed The Side Of The Blade   47

New   49

Automatic Reception   50

Affair   51

Flight   52

Are you Young?   55

Addict   56

I Knew A Girl Once   57

Once I Had   58

She Kissed Her Lips   59

Mating Wings   60

The Request Denied   61

It's You, You I Crave, To Eat   62

Reunion   65

Arrow   66

The Unmediated Crime   67

When We Leave   68

Youth   69

Scaly Enemy, Time   70

Where Are The Masters   71

The Melodious Child   72

Mercury Protoplasm   73

When The Earth Was   74

That Night The Moon   76

And So Left Here In Retreat   78

Comparisons   81

Reverent Pause   82

Look Where The Search To Learn   83

And To The Morning Flight   86

Dream Talk   89

This Barking War Of The Sun   90

Body & Spirit   91

The Call   92

Why This Constant Urge To Apologize   93

Reunion, Reunite   94

An Evening Sky's Hoarse Whine   95

In The Beginning   96

Rattle Through   97

Nostalgia   98

Shh…   99

Carry Legends   100

Yet Nothing Is Left Undone   101

Where Are They Taking Us   102

Ancient Songs She Sang   103

What Do I Want?   104

The Past And Future   105

Then There Was   106

A Calm Look Is Thrown Backwards   107

Sun   108

You Are The One   111

The Sun Came   112

Mystery Upon Mystery   113

"I've Felt For A Long Time Now"   114

Climb The Cliffs Of Spring   115

Shaman's Passing   116

Exit & Entry   118

You See There Is Not The Slightest   119

What Have We Forgotten   120

Scattered Witnesses   123

The Great Gift Has Slowed   125

The Trouble Is   126

Even When Fever Incarnate   127

In The Dry Laughter   128

As The Long Temple Road   130

Songs In Pieces   132

Empty Hands Etc.

Inspiration   135

When The Day Slips   136

In Plotting My Course   139

Take The Appraisal   140

Give Over the Strong   141

When The Animals Arrive again   142

Dwindling Pools At Last Of Madness   143

In The Green Sirocco   144

Honored Quiet House   145

Out Of The Darkness   146

Now That The Mask Is Full   147

Night/Descending Hour   148

The City Sleeps   149

Only Beside The Cold Remains   150

Youth Uncared For   151

Of Lie-Dressed Lives   152

Age   153

Worn Thin From The Inside Out   154

The Vision Too Is Mortal   155

FRAGMENTS

Involuntary Secrets

159-188

Free the connections and tones of the past,
new compositions await us with anxious pageantry.

MESSENGER OF THE CROWS

SEPARATION

Time again to flee the town
time again to walk the forest
beside the cool brooding stride
of the spirits' fragrant wealth.
Into the night
and the quick bosom
of circling secret creatures
stretching for the heat.

Under the arc
    we have been sent
  with joyless christening
    and in wondrous
      discomfort to produce
the worth of our lives,
    the evidence of which
to be laid like hunted
    rabbit before the
  banquet council and
there judged ripeningly
    in accordance
with our efforts
    and sympathy
for those we held along the way.

CITY

cool seductress
brute steel sustenance
the pant of traffic
ethnic symphony
dry sister Atlantis

cruel manacled remembrance
webbed captive shielded prototype forest
autonomy of nonspace
autonomy of season and year
safe mistrust clutched dagger
fear the boundary of the circle
and lack of viny verdure to grow
over the eyelids like cobwebs
fear the hidden glow of the mistress sphere
and quick numbness

To have left
the caravan
and struck off
on our own
to forage
for the feast
we have missed
all along

Achievements
to blend in the fire
with the ash of prayers
    and hope

The moon—
cat's eye
silver talon
scripture
and map

swift robed
the crooked princess
dwarf streaming
red streamers in her hair
kiosk lips
limp night air, presume
hungry risk
stare the stars into a fevered guide

Porpoise hills
The sea earth
Quick restive tranquility
Fleeting blood connection
Leaf priest and mirror ground
Stirred clouds
Absence of the sea queen
Sadness crowns like night

Ghosts and dreams
in dawn's mercury
circle about the
velvet chamber
sniffing sharply
snarling at one another
in accusations of sadness

To be a Slavic warrior
veined in bulk
souvenirs of the river-people
tangled about the waist
nomadic in my bed
fresh fur for the winter
a quick flint resting
along the blade
faithful spark beneath
canopy stars
and meat smoke

NIGHT

Great inky masked
Hallowed
Corrupt angel disciple

Lean accommodations
for the miracle
and the rose
and the valley of idols
resting stony in
offshore realms
lengthy, desperate

CLOUD

Scaly wintry Chinese-dragon cloud
threads thinly among the cathedral
peaks smoking me toward where the
shore waits and the sea is rose
bleed splendor and feather warm—
a vast anonymous assembly of smiles
that, when connect, alchemize into
a giant lovesoul floating vellum
island ah embrace.

Full of corridors, eager to hatch
the horrors ranged along neighboring
hills, which look like reclining
heads of girls, the dreamers
stretch their hands into the mist
and receive horrible fists of
waiting, dripping sand, the
slide of time

"When is the swooping hour!"

Demise ensues calm order.
The nature of the hills is to
    carry us west
into the unknown slope
and the raven's daughter winged
    with surprise.

I will leave poor and will remain
    poor
but I'll have my songs, and pure.

STORM

Lightning
throbbing pyramid of no-sound

Then a slow snaking of
rumble through the long sky
"I have found it!"

"What?"

"My lostness, I've found it!
It's in that roll of thunder
I can just glimpse the back
of its wings receding in a flash
with the sound.
It's like the final flap of a
stingray's hands as it
disappears into the murk.

O I'm so happy, I *found* it!
O I've found it."

Murky children along the river with
    primitive weapons.
Dragonfly horde, innocuous wing
    symphony.
Black mass of swallows crown circling
sharks about the church's high
silhouetted roof in insect frenzy;
thundercloud arms embrace the
crucifix peaking its shadow into dusky
    penetration.

The walk of night advances to break
    like a bell.

I'm amazed by sight—
I remember that

Dance for me
Let me see you dance
Let me see the colors of
your skirts whirl,
your legs separate
and teeth gleam

ANCIENT

Beautiful and tortured the Indian slumped
upon the river's current. Thirty feet high
he mountained from the surface as the waves
buoyed and worked in black loops like eels
between his toes. The droop of his head
was the enchanted hand of a star. The dark
seaweed of his braids lapped the golden chrome
of his chest and sullenly dipped their paintbrush
ends away from the spear jetting up from the
water and poised against the thick ball of his
shoulder, lifting into heaven a giant icicle for
the nipple suck of angels.

    Silent and still he stood sleepy guarding
the night, the air about him a shield, a movie
screen.

    And as the boat of pale camera-clutching
mortals sniffed past his feet—a soundless
pregnant mouse wary to wake the cat—no
disturbance stirred the blue night, no wordy
action churned the electricity. Our admiration
sailed into the might of his weariness.

PRELUDE (News of Departure)

That day
   the clouds were
   supple Bali dancer's hands
    smiling with danger

ghost in the iris
the shroud in the eyelid

Loose the body from the boat!

Wagging temples
the worship of eyes
crawling hills

gifts

splendid architecture

tales of smoky magic
mating
sexual insinuations
and tame snake advancement
tales of lake vastness
trading
open-thighed villages
color

The carriage lurches on
bearing us with it trailing dead
purple pigeons and ivory anchors,
supple facsimiles of each passing
moment, sarcastic gifts to Time.

Small gifts enable adventure
The hero lies westward
in a well-marked place

Now who will be the next
to plunder dawn's promise
and inspire the miracle
of perfect abundance

Drought trails us
The herd drifts into newly
burned meadows

Smoldering roots

We
      are
            ready!

Dog vision
Wolf watch
Phantom celebration
Ceremony

Make the fathers visible
Interpret the cloud people

Thunder

Dance like thunder

ASCENT

Whispering women shrouded at
    the crossway
their mingling voices snake like
night wind in trees, like slow
dark dreams portentously writhing
unraveling the long coil of the brain,
marching the ghost back to the
place of conception.

Born of fire
Left to wander
Take the wind
and memorize the power
brought to plunder soft senses
grown fat with realized ambition

In the becoming of the hollow
of our innocence golden is the
tear that washes over our lives;
warm gentle voices of the myths
build parables and spiraling
    towers in the wind
in honor of our returning.

Reentering the lights of town
bathed in the cool of peril
carrying songs and psalms and
warnings from the surge toward
    transcendence
I tell you again
of visions of the moon
and of all the tangled feasts
built to embody her
to receive her promise of lurid
    lyric perfection

OF MEN AND MONSTERS

Lying lawlessly along the moon's tracks,
    the eyelid lifting sleep's stone,
  I recognize the rush of the beastly
breeze and the foundlings returning in it
    dragging watery remains
  of dream's roam and run.

Ah the liberties excessively grown
    in the legs of darkness.
Families migrate from dross boundaries,
    fool's gold,
  and return to the trees, nestle in the bodice
    of nature's breath.
Whole novels are read within
    the texture of the skin.
Blue aromas of steaming roll from
    the flesh emptying the dregs of memory,
  ravishing endless mansions
        magnificently hidden.

Do you know what it is
that holds us at
the bounds of the yard,
away from the other arrivals,
pensive at the leery muse freshness
    of the burial?

Do you know what leaves us
longing to wear the white satin flame
and the cool buttoned cloud?

Do you know the warped velvet
    in laughter
the psychotic cackle in listening
the warmth of a stare?

Do you know the stirring flash of
a new connection with a primitive
    thought?

Systematic
descent. Each
level unique
hatchings of separation.
I feel it
now, I feel the sudden
terror of
what it means to be
alive and
vast,
the struggle to end the film
life after life
with a smile;
I feel the swirl evil leaving my finger ends and opening.
I claim
the rifting sizzle drip of the moon
as my companion
and the rise and fall of
the heartbeat's
tide to be the only true music—
and I

open.

with open eye and open mouth
we move, steady wavering
deeper into the hot throat chasm
further past the curling beckon
    of the tongue
closer to the light of the end of
    the first half
and still we haven't uncovered
the self's precursor laws unmonitored
highway illusion of border pure
    seeping
nor have we tried

the duty to learn the language of
    the direction of the works
duty to metamorphose into symbol
    assemblers
duty to gather the forces of the
night and the day and learn
their tongue and intentions and
how they perpetrate and endure
the immensity of such broad
antique space and unique lodgings

Meat tooth, Time, slow
growing rags and fits of
hunger, how's all this
going to end?
    As it began, without
    consent in a dark damp
    place, lonely and afraid
    with just this one question:
    Have I done all I could?

SYMPTOMS

Dead flower vigil

Human intricacies fed by the
snare of voices

Moon sobbings in the gloom of
morning radiance

Loose night syllables

Hair, a nest of shiny rope

Payphone receiver, the slap of perfume

The sun running on centipede legs

Veins tubing at the temples of an old
man, hands ravaged with the storm of
slow knowing

Paint scraped sky

The remembrance of trees

The smell of dog birth

Splattered tshirt and sleek shins, sweaty

backseat parking

In the cinematic rotunda of memory
I am lord and this is my time in Time—
I'm determined to love it

To live
    To touch
To
    TOUCH!

To caress and consume through
    the pores and hammer of
        fingertips
To seek marble skin, velvet and
    stone, fur
silk entrails of water,
    wood fiber
the flight in cool air and
    dry heat suffocation

To Touch!
    To Live!

A willingness to welcome all
degrees of the flame

A call to darkness, call
    to innocence,
Back to the womb, inner world
    the deep
Sleep, friendly dagger, posture
of the voice of comely reptile
    radiance,
abundance agile clarity,
wine of the world
line of a girl
to die in the whirl
séance flavor
and the stink of morning forgotten

I will follow you to
your slow flowering
leaping whirling
in naked rooms
as your eyes
pout sensual requests,
opulent secrets to the runes

Return, clash
with the fire girl
fire wand
fire walls of warning

Rooted in mystery
Slow ascent of awakening
Her tunnel takes you home
to the belly
to the circle of wind, the hoop
    the power,
to the source of milk

Breeding season
The long advance
Spring has come
to lead us into its hot
tunnel

Flowery beasts fed on semen
and sweat
and the sweet swift dissolve
promise of the world dangling
like a prize hunk of meat

Somber casings
Maiden corners
untouched and dirty
rival the wanting
Smooth shapely legs
sit nearby and lead
upward to the garden return

I refuse the invitation

There is secret unnamed
business I must attend
in my own earthly garden mess

Beauty embraces
Love breathes
Cassandra screams—

"This is the day the world stops!"

MATING TRICK

To offer something
unconsciously separate
from all the rest
of the beauty

To dip a tongue's
length into the cavity
of the showman and
somehow make it authentic

To regard rabid
change as terse calculation
and rebuild the blocks
of the personality

To become a great
well-oiled yea-sayer

Terror chased her
as she opened her eyes
in the morning silver,
    temple of dawn
Ravaged seeker, lavish visitor
in the shallow grave

She woke with scars of tears
    down her face
beside her lover, the huntsman
who was crouched in a lion pose
reading to her from
The Book Of Years
filled with regrets voids and
    fears,
unfulfillment

"Is this really all we have?"
she asked
"There must be more, to be sure—
but where is it! Where's the
magic we always suspected?
I WANT TO BE MAGIC!"

―――――――――

He placed the side of the blade
against her face and ran
it coolly along the curve of
her cheek and on down,
resting it beneath her chin

It's cold, he told her
Feel it

Don't—
Don't scare me, she whispered,
and took him to bed

He rose to leave

No, I want you to stay

I know you do

He fastened his belt
shook his antlers in the gloom
and walked from the sulfurous
glow of her chamber into the
conquering night, a monster
large for the stars whose mysteries
he burned to write and teach

Find God in your dreams!

He cried to the sleeping town
Climb to Him hailed on an
island of severed raven heads!
His island is your safe idle beds

NEW

Richly now we turn to each other
the caverns of ourselves
and offer what we can to displace
the singularity of the artifacts
weighing in our throats

Richly now we save for each other
the glow of bodily compare

Automatic reception

In bed she flutters tears
and butterfly kisses upon my cheek

It's all too easy to accept
while the dream still tumbles
downhill into apologetic slumber

"This is not the life I would have chosen!"

Return, cling to the moon's skirt
take the path to the high hilly
garden where lonesome visitors
are left at ease to breathe their
art and dream the walk of their lives

Back to the willow haunt
Back to craving
Back to dry restless appraisal
and heated animal straying

the hunt

AFFAIR

Should I
leave you
Should I
believe you
What if I
deceive you
Will that make
me love you
again

FLIGHT

Changing landscape
Changing mindscape
A shadow lays across the earth
and forges a boundary of new will

A passageway collapses
as a new route is born

**There's a lot of distance between you and me.
How do I get to where you are?**

Are you young?
Are you—
young?

No cops
No stops

Dead and dying

Alive

The curl of your smile
is my adventure
Toward the temple shore of your
inarticulate city I descend
A bag full of deities to disperse,
dispense, and disrobe

Ah honey it's all for you—
you and I
The mock and lock and
laugh of the world
dancing on tiny feet like
raindrops

ADDICT

Her hair is thrown across
Cinnamon divide
Whips me frothy into
    religious surveillance

Everything good is escaping

The clock is no more than
    ejaculatory twitchings
The clouds, three-dimensional gold
    sagging of ribbon
The sudden voices and shadows
    like black flies that keep
startling me are only my
    wild breath
There is nothing beyond
    that can move me more
than the silken bridge of her hair,
    and the way summer nibbles her toes
into grimacing jewels
    and smoothes unreal her skin

How do I leave her? How do I
ever leave such mad apathetic beauty?

I knew a girl once who kept
a knife by her bed.
We never made it, we'd just
masturbate next to each other
on the bed and then afterwards
confess it was the greatest
sex on earth.

O yeah, the knife? It didn't
bother me—long brown-handled
butcher's knife—I knew it was
only for those who wouldn't
let her masturbate next to them.

Once I had
    a love so fair
So loved to twine
    red worms
        in my beard
And did all she could
    to make me scream
        and sulk

I loved her very much

And to this day
    I can't forget
How I followed
    through upon
        my threat
Leaving her to
    the inhabitants
        of the gulch

And I still love her very much

She kissed her lips
to his ear
and spoke
like a seashell

The rain has passed, she hissed
follow me back to the chateau

I will allow you foul torture
and the key to the place
of delicious seizure—
I keep it hidden among
my books
beside the parrot's house
and the piranha's swim
and the golden scented lamp

I want my windows thrown

open with pain
I want to fly over cool
wrinkled faces of mountains
caged in the eagle's meat hooks

MATING WINGS

It's as if we
came into the world
together, like two halves
of a dream.
I can't just dismiss that

And what would you have
me do? Just roll over
and forget my life?
No. I won't.

Why must we come at
each other like fists!
Take me to your room,
take me home,
tame me.

I'll be good, wait and see—
see how I've changed.
My eyes have softened.
See? Look how they've softened.

You can't play me like
some fat cat belly!

The request denied
antlered love tears the
bucking night
How to receive the night
in lust?
How to relieve the life
chosen from resigned loss?

The connecting shadow once
black as conspiracy, now
fading, takes the nightcloth
close to let our penetration
pervade the swell of nothing,
except the blurry drifting canal
remembrance of lovers' hands young
in the rain

It's you, you I crave, to eat,
the fruit bite bright nibble
of your throat, ear, the rich
birdie valley of your belly,
the earth roll of your green
hips to lavender to ease
rollicking forward, the teeth
gleam bit of your breasts
rising in a chant of pillows
majesty mountain sunbeam
marshmallow peaks and I glide,
I glide...over your dew meadow...
    long...

Trials and revelations
Death and resurrection
Rebirth and transformation

REUNION

Back from beyond
The wild kingdom
Royal labyrinth
Kiss if the sun

Shall we collide
and dream we are one,
divine deeper things lost
in the presence of one another,
the pressure of our hearts
beating each other into
foreign rhythms

ARROW

No more concessions
   in the spinning flight
I am whole now
   I intend to remain whole
and find my own leafy landing—
   when I land

I am brutal assurance
My eyes house no receding
The guard wrestles no shadow
When they see me they will say
   He's changed!
And my new beard will sparkle
   and raise into bristling coolness
      and a smile
   and black—
it'll still be black

The unmeditated crime
Divine possession
Liberation opens its legs on
    small couches of abandon
Deft delicate surge
Mobility in restriction
The kingdom caged in the
    ribs is torn across and
        exposed
Glory mops its forehead
Ruins are renovated after
    the fire and set asunder

Blessed freedom
Bloody freedom
You will pay later
Now is favor
Now lives forever buried
in blinking symptoms
    of romance

When we leave
this fine dragging fury
let us not miss
immortality
nor weep for
the one we could not have

Let's rather bend
to the shore like fawns
and wave back
a smile
to those who
still cling to the joke

YOUTH

Frozen, gutted—
surely this ragged spirit
cannot offend.
Sleek beasts slump in corners
lolling tongues at each other in
the machinery of night.
Cruel fixtures of time
losing the battle for excitement,
rutting, stunted.

Scaly enemy, Time
The moment in hiding
The cold waking death-walk
Long line of lusty faceless hearts
Lost in designed slither descent

Where are the masters,
the garden watchers, our
soft copious daughters who
lead away from spoiled streams?
Are they asleep in the weeds?
Flustered and intertwined
in the underworld?

They are needed here afloat
in the mortal common image
coaching enterprise, to
strengthen the ride of the
raven which carries our
uncertain passion in its
mystery mouth shine.
They are needed once again
to minister through the
in-and-out nightmare
with the righteous discomfort
of labyrinthine eyes, to
stay us astride lunar weeping
and all the things
strange waking
refuses to allow.

THE MELODIOUS CHILD

What is in your head?

I don't know,
it's all like a movie, the child said.
I am loose footed
tracking rape across the dawn,
tracing paradox gouged
from the very beginning into
the walls of my eyes.
I have only enough time to
clear the soil from them, the
soil of my birth, when my
eyes become filled again,
become deep level gardens again—
of potential,
always *potential*.

Mercury protoplasm
the first light of creation
first deaf spark in the
    leaden water sphere
soon enclosed by the map of veins
and flesh of reason
too hidden in the warm source

(There's a curious feeling
That our lives, our every
Action has been mysteriously
Mapped-out upon the fishy globe)

We must protect the power of this
small light, our companion—
mustn't let industrious lusting
or good humor or the sadness
of old women seize her

When the earth was
young and full
and not melting
and the blood of
time did not pool
in our hands—
when we were rife
and timeless and
enchanted in our
dusky blind evening
acre before the blade
of the plow was
set down—
when the thrillful feather
of sleep did not seduce
or tickle us and
feathery we slept in
tender husks of myth
trapped coil of innocence
before the world had
jaws and dutiful clutches
dutiful smiles
dirty eyes and
routine miles
we needed not
seek the kingdom
so vehemently.

Back then it was
the skill of truth.

———————————

That night the moon
rose bloody out of
the lake and spoke
to no one, but me—
and I'm not talking

The child's game
left us is a tantrum
and the camel goddess
fell in love with her enemy,
    the rider

Everyone knew it was gonna happen

The forgetful angel played an
untamed fury on the water
and danced way too long

The scholar left in brooding disgust
The rest of us didn't know *how*
    to respond
We kinda liked it though
Exercise through observation and swollen
    outbursts of fear

We held no special incantation
but the night was a success,
a small corner of wilderness

Secret lunar possession

And so left here in retreat
steeped in honor
swarmed with the battle for a
   new belief
a beggar
lustful alone
comes to me the magic theater
               *
      *   *

A foul-aired feast
Naked and bloated
the cripple in the corner
shriveled humbling fruit
enemy reminder
eyes bleeding for life
sunken vacuum halls of horror
all laughter suffers his cure

A young jackal nurses at the
   favored nun
Black and white bulbous streaks
   of charity
A low cooing murmur wraps
the room in delirium
Opium incense
Plush velveteen drapery

Bordello fixtures

Squirming groaning gropes
Falling wigs
Violet smoke
Masks
A dream of leather
Hoods
and black lashing gloves
Gigantic silhouettes paint the
walls with lewd crimson movement

A new car arrives
Fresh blood
Red plumes
Flowing scarlet screams that fly
and twist into giant flailing sperm

Hooves and high heels

Bull horns

Knives and capes and daffodils
Gold teeth
Eyes like watch faces
Creaking oiled clothes

"Who's the virgin?
Who'll be the savior this time?"

"He left"

"Couldn't cut it eh? The little prick"

"I could almost taste the stew too.
Shoulda seen him, he'da made a
great soup bone. Even the goat
liked him. Kept a little dead red
bird in his hair for luck"

Red runny death
A play and place for voices like Time
The widowed soul finds solace, rest
in this velvet chamber, this wigged-out
mortuary

Wolf watch
Phantom celebration
Ceremony
Receive dog vision in a wet jungle dream
and dance like thunder

———————————

COMPARISONS

And the smooth stretch of skin
And the curve of a banister
And the side of a candle
And the sponge sense of a marigold
And oaken veneer
And polished lacquer
And the rub of teeth
And the slicking of an eyebrow
And the neon tube
And the death in feathers
And the wink burning in the leveling of dusk

Reverent pause for the
harbinger hanged

He dared speed art's conclusive
　　　progression
Its final and most logical end
Humbly showing the essence of what
it's been getting at all along

Lucidly inspired the artist
dressed a gallery with mirrors

Look where the search to learn
passion has led us,
trailing rumpled hearts and
torn wars, banner skulls—
troubled flags of our waking
Secrecy and sadness surrounds us
like the language of insects

To have come wandering from
the soft-scented hour with
beast-curled hair wondering
if this is real is little enough

To have stepped out from behind
the shadow's tower
and entered the sail of the choir
has been our pleasure and disgust
But the obligation continues

Treasure loss
Loose threads
Our lives the laugh of making
Birth, the miss of every approach,
opened its snarl and left a lair
of moments to be lengthened
and inserted into the wide growling lake
growing dim with midnight midlife youth

showing shaken in the flight
into the dark reward
of all our days

Is there a message to possess
in the regret of coming,
retrace?
A simple word like fear says so much

When the eyes of certainty are
unbalanced and clean to reach
to dream and full, sagging,

buxom for the whole gallery and
the sift sculpture swirl
the calling and search seem clear

It's all a search,
one tender jump after another
to the next flower spike-oozed
stand of fire

The ranch is raging
Cautious hour
I've fallen for the lash of torment

A fine device to hold at bay
love and life

More and more
the bow to become

the tornado-headed fool,
to hold to self

and the network haunt and whole therein
for the splendid torture of artful
propagation,
the ache to remain large in the
thighs of dream.
Fear of the trap
Fangs of labor

Tender

In dream it's best.
In sleep we speak to each other,
a thousand wings climb from
our bodies, raise us up
Our selves define
inch the vine that ties our halves,
one universe
Destiny, the jewel widely displayed
to the keeping, is enhanced before us

This gem, weeping blaze
puzzle game
to laugh and make the maze
our own

And to the morning flight of
    spirits,
hosts of sparrows exploded from
    cottony-dawn ivy,
I release all custom and glory

The sun walks in with bloody shoes

DREAM TALK

—Have you ever slept someplace where you don't know where the hell you are?

—You mean physically?

—No…

This barking war of the sun
This looming this slow
eating away of the nerves
like the infiltration of a
    criminal's fingers

BODY & SPIRIT

Messenger of the crows
Warring heads
Belly dancers
Blood
Passion
Invisible means
The source and search
Inward
The feast
The flow
The unraveling moon

THE CALL

Strange translations
Disturbing images from across
the dark shore
Eyes like weary torches
masked and mad in the insect night
The monk in the moon
The sun-sucked sea

I've been to the forest,
knelt at the alter of the streams,
cursed the day on fire,
and of all things I feel it best
I leave and attend a vision
of life through the grave

Why this constant urge to apologize
for my life
Darkness forest
World of fire
Original experience
Blue bubble floating from the cracked skull
Fleeing spirit
Fleeing the field of Time
Shackle King
Body

I dream black whirling birds through
the drink of their sky

Reunion, reunite
Refusal to mourn further
    forming prayers, out there
        in the mist of reality

Lone participant in a drama
    of history, words, and
        silent religious reverie
Playing a secret game all by myself
    and losing

An evening sky's hoarse whine
New moon like wet revival,
    sopping penetration
New explorers of consciousness
Pale cavern births
Monuments, places of towering
death, sacred atrocities
Textural evangelists
Neon
And sacred gestures

Moving through history with a
necessary sense of illusion,
    immortality

In the beginning
as in the end
no distinction of sex
no births, no deaths

A licking of the mouth
One word
One universe
Single concurring network of flame

Rattle through
The windy skeleton
Childhood
Clean bones of the past

NOSTALGIA

The scent remains
keeping the story of ourselves alive
like the talk of children
alone in a midnight backyard tent

Shh…
Hey…Hey listen…Listen…
Battle wings
The sigh of growth
The long slow stretch
of times fingers like blades
cutting us down

Carry legends to
rivers of union
What lies beyond
love is something
commonly animal—
and beyond that
there is merely faith
and conjecture
and strong abandon

Yet nothing is left undone.
The dogs of winter,
white roaming packs
hot on the heels,
the endless meat season
turning in the belly of
the grave again and again,
the waking and the birth,
the slow resurgence of the
recognition of the symbols
dripping with secrets and memories,
faithless and flowering,
the thought, the dream of thought,
the dream, empty and alive
we enter and leave done, done.

Where are they taking us
distant jungle rhythms
night aflower

Where does it end
this misery
this longing
this hope
the long subtle murder

Where is the entrance to the
one fine peaceful place
if not in your arms

Ancient songs she sang
Her eyes asked
What is your life?

A feeling of being
overwhelmed, aware,
and not quite sure of
anything…cept uh,
things are not as
they should be

What do I want?

Disappearance—
into the smile horizon
the breath of smoke
the sparkle eye of love

What do I want?

To live beyond the mask

The past and future,
phantasmagoria—
Life's tragedy

The words *I wish* are the
saddest human utterance

Then there was the
storm, the loss of
beauty, and we wept
for Time—and we knew.
We knew then with
all our hearts that
there would always
be loss, and we would
be lost, and the hope
and thought of living,
truly living, is merely
    conjecture.

A calm look is thrown backwards
in this drama

The wronged citizen crawls
from the sea and churches
plead for light
The flood has not yet
reached our parents' farm
but they'll soon see the new
true strength and gain
respect for mystical experiences—
they'll realize our pursuits were
correct and why they shall never
see us again on this side
of the wind

Sun
Moon
Father
Mother

Unfathomable the depths
that lurk to ties us together

**You don't travel too far away
from your body, do you?**

You are the one
to sing of the birth
You are the one
to tell us of our worth

O divine lusty hammered herald
save our poor planet,
save our poor population flung
too far away from the initiates
　　of the sun
alive, dying

They've gives us life, murdered us

The sun came
through the trees
like angel wings
gentle reminder
speaking peace
in the language
of the birdcall

Emerald spirits
made an alter
at the floor
of the forest
where sunrays
fell their warm sighs

Already the chant
had begun from
the hillside—

"It's alright
   We're all here
It's alright
   We're all here…"

And there was dancing

Mystery upon mystery
The age of magic
The black summit
Wishing at death through
the minion of innocent play

"I've felt for a long time now,"
she said once, "that I'm
and old soul."

Well of course we are all old
souls, the trouble is most have
a problem with recollection,
remembering in the blind light
the ancient symbols and their
assembly. We're all tasty ghosts
passing through the meaty jaws of
Time again and again.

The hawk or swallow
eagle or dove hangs in the air
weaves the sky into matting
and shades the sun

Climb the cliffs of spring
Double face of horror
   and beauty
Black summit
New beginning

There must be a SACRIFICE!

SHAMAN'S PASSING

At the first familiar fragments
of death a catalog of life—
moments, inspirations, images,
the feeling of in and out

A story of new ancestors
surrounds him with pleasure
of the palace
    It begins:
"Praise night
the final season, the beginning"

Tear's come to the eye like
insects in a hard black crunch
and jump out falling to the
ground like watermelon seeds

A supplication is turned inward
to call for the last time the
beasts heavy with the sweat of
    guidance

Will they come?

Soon he will be as they are,
an animal of light,
communicating with those on

this shore through small
sparks of electricity
or weeping drizzle of
fireworks
He will be invisible as
time wasted with uncertainty

EXIT & ENTRY

There are only three things I want to tell you

Be true to yourself, for only you are god.
Life is continual expanse. Never be completely
satisfied, complacent, always stay open—for
he who remains empty will always be filled.
And finally, watch nature. Attend the seasons
and trees, all animate and inanimate things
of nature—they will teach you; then do whatever
necessary to stay close to this knowledge, your
soul, for today it is easily seduced away.

You see, there's not the slightest
resistance left in me.
I am a ribbon of stream
bending myself to the contour
of the landscape.
I will hold you
as I shape
myself around you
in avoidance.

What have we forgotten?

Satyrs and maidens
Garden Heaven
Lovely infiltration of the
lady of the beasts
laying roses over
hazy mountain meadows
Many-god minded eyes
open for any new favor
or promise of peace

**Bend closer to the light, she said.
I want to see your face glow like owl eyes.**

Scattered witnesses
of the new sun,
long dreamers of
natural observance,
faith,
believers in islands of rebirth
and elderly faces of the moon
I call to thee
from the swirl of the night
I call on the
gathered majesty of your
singing desert circle,
vigil ecstasy

Ordeal silence
and separation
and quiet tribal knowledge
leads the senses summery
into lean sultry curious
animal refinement

Brotherhood abounds
in echoes of the trees
and the summit casts
down its cloud of
blue beard
summoning ascent

to snowy wells
and skyward coitus on
heavenly tongues
with watchful spirits
of the myths

The great gift has slowed
and blurred in tilted statue cave waking
and at each moment of delicate
rising I wait and cry: What do we do? Now
where do we place the quiet fire?

The action of repose
attractive in the daywell
where action has lost its luster
to find to foster the wolving
of delusion grows giants
in the cloud of the head
knifes ambition in the bed
of its sweat and tells all—
all is one wind hollow.

The trouble is
to find an experience
that makes us feel alive
and cling to it ecstatic connection
like mouthing the monster—
Time's breast.
To wrestle the sword from
its sheath and advance howling
toward the shrouded kingdom,
the church-chested flesh, to
rescue worship from the impotent,
the social club, and restore
the metaphor, gentle sanctified
    forest,
the path of the sun,
bull's blood,
fruit of the vine.
The silence has not left us.
Its mystery is our core.

Even when fever incarnate
acts upon its rage
and the little earth of man
revolves in his skin
and the winding world of the brain
tightens the labyrinth's walk
around a single secret destiny that
refuses to give its face to the
firelight of this world
I am safe and full-membered equipped
in the soft wound of the search,
well on my way to the last wheel turn
trip of the meat season, gold as green.

In the dry laughter
tumbling over us
like bloodless consultation,
in the strong fading of summer,
in the pained ringing chorus of singed
guardian hills worn thin with stolen
pleasure, graffiti fire holiday,
strange in sleep and drunk with dream
the raging of blank desire persists
in the last of memory.

This is the last obsession
born on the back of black
supple wings
this is cool and bright
and perfect tradition
sideshow wishes awaiting admission
to the fiery jaunt mixing in
the pit where legends breed.

What great bounty
shall be forced
when the life has spread
like extinguished sapphire
against the rivers of night?

The thunder has battled

the silence slept
creamy, beauty rose, stripped
from the white horses of the sea
and surveyed the warm thought
of pardon against the
hollow-lighted town.

Dreamy, beauty spoke, ripped
from the warm web of her sleep
and told wind from the wounds
of the old war: Man and Time,
and Time's battalion
wearing away the footprints
beneath our feet
and the bone at our door.

As the long temple road
opens to slumber
and the night invites
a reckless grin still with hunger
    and cold,
still aching at the wait,
we reach deeper into doubt
and the faithless kingdom.

The garden hides from sightless
    dwellers.
Murder occurs at birth and after
when eyes are too much like glass,
and a low red glow grows through
the trees of the fleshly globe,
the source and search,
hidden princely rage pondering
    worth
and the race from the curtained
    certain future.

The world is too much with us.
Walk the walls of the labyrinth
to kiss its inhabitant
and recite the gold behind the eyes.

True meaning is secret among us.

Release from greed
the tangled beast in the skin,
take him back to the bank of symbols,
skeleton key,
humble in the hands
of the gambol of the gods.

———————

Songs in pieces
Torn and winged
We die
An armful of signals waving
at the sun to stop the long
bloody march of its November
    face
betrays our procession

What is to be gained by the
steady accumulation of habits
and respite and cold luxury
ambition is awash already in
the full belly of the grave
and its bloated thinking

We have only to become
    perfection mistaken
We have only to caress ourselves
    in the fire
We have only to dance with
the monkey of our hearts till
we fall from the edge of
    this dream

EMPTY HANDS ETC.

INSPIRATION

In the food of letters
spilling a bit in relief
from the dry corners of the
feast lingering and the awkward
    dance
the guide of unearthly streams
steps from her spiteful hiding
and extends at last a hand
out of the darkness toward
the passage and color of
    deliverance

When the day slips
into a more thick and
bloodier pair of hands
mute fingers
and the sky cracks
its black smile like
an ever widening pupil
panther claw
plush raven fur
then the dream slowly
begins to awaken
rise and take form
beside the silent waiting presence
of doomed expectation

I left
I had to wrestle with my eagle

In plotting my course
I have left you alone
with your cat stretching
silence along the furniture
waiting for the work
to pass into the word
of a drowned Christ—
or something

Take the appraisal of the long
severed withered sky
and leave the wisdom memory
of her face to float the dark
ravaged turns of the stream.
Your hands now are not
the same as those that once
smoothed their route over
her carnival flesh, breathing,
clawing handfuls of lean
lusty moments, devoured
against the devouring of Time.

Give over the strong
diversity of strength
to captive resistance
and stand against the
world wake the flood
the flow of brutal
skull-crossed longing
and stiffening fear.
Give over the breath
of hiding the tangled
message in the kiss
the politics of speaking
the loneliness of simply
sitting still beside
quiet rhythms of the
great quivering curtain
anxious to rise to reveal
the emptiness of its prize
darkly and familiar wavering.
Give over the moment's funeral
and leave us to the scent
prying beneath the open grave,
the route the mouth
the cave entrance of
eternal wonder, restless.

When the animals arrive again
from jeweled pastures and black
flights, unions, hot far-out
countries, and speak to us with
their silence of internal glory
and radiance and wide melting purity
then I will gather the seasons in
my fist and we shall head for that
faintest hidden hint of a smile at
the edge of the moon and plant our
rainy flag in the naked kiss of the
world with a slam of the door
and a "Fuck You All!"
and give birth to the life
of the prayer

Dwindling pools at last of madness
overstretched and lasting along
the wild highway, wilderness and
the sullen advance, the whisper,
the pull toward ambivalent ends,
fate's monster disguised as self
drags himself onward from
the forest door, across the
sunken heights and night's jungle,
to the glory and pawn of
the face of her.

Bright thrown descent.

In the green sirocco of
your eyes, desert song
and ripe ember glow,
shrouded armies advance,
windbrushed dunes spray
like savage flame in
an enchanted whirl,
mild incantation,
wild dog-toothed gathering,
surrounded,
benediction and unruly
    captured house

Honored quiet house
Lion's nest
Mating retreat
Innocuous words empty
the heart of its
tight defenses in a
black melted stream
and populate the
aviary of the senses
with silent squatting
demons smiling with
confused solace
while nestling down
into unfamiliar satisfaction

Out of the darkness
unknown spires struggle
swirling toward the stars
and the silent milky light
cradled there
Crowned wisdom
Empress throne
Cruel heights

Breaking from the darkness
unknown spires push upward,
waiting for the rest to
follow, waiting for the rest
to shrug the night
and match the blind grope
of their climb, to rise
above the snake wall
and peer over to see the
golden smile of the horizon
waiting…waiting

Now that the mask is full
and splitting at the seams
sympathy will fall like
a rain of roses,
and all of us who have
picked up the charge and
taken our positions beside
resilient towers, personal
and divine, will soon
proclaim that the war
has been correct
and the tally of the dead
a proper number

NIGHT

Descending hour
bring again your
slavish romance
luxury of the senses
bring once more
your velvety blue posture
and remove the terrible
haunting slumped like
cadavers in the brooding
corners of our minds

Your darkening face
your conquering weight
smother us with your
anonymous pleasure
to restore our faith
in the coming ease
of the awaited end

The city sleeps
in a drowning dream.
Naked, the rush of Time
tears through the streets
unhitching crucified desires
from dull lampposts and
dark rooftops and wet bridges
and tucks them away deep in
the tomb of unused lives.

All saints perish.

Only beside the cold remains
of the city's fallen children
does the night take comfort and
    companion.
Beside the spinning blotted stars,
beside the fresh long fog-wrapped
    cadaver in the gutter,
beside hard remote women
withering like arctic flowers,
fresh to see the languor and
the language and the cool
knowledge of the rough throbbing
rhythm transformation of the
spirit of the night, slow in sacrifice

She rises

Youth uncared for
unseen
trampled to death
in the mad rush for its capture

Only the hard dark treasure
awaits
only the return
only unseen passages
and loose portrayals
and glorious folly
will welcome our advance

Of lie-dressed lives and youth
fleshed with warm dream
Time making skeletons of us all
lays us in the lap of wild
harlot ruin and the mean
certain city laugh of contagious
    prophesy

With the lean approach of autumn
closing in like taught ribs
our ships are full and drowning
with cries of the lonesome dead
awaiting desperately our swift
arrival from the table of the
    devouring

AGE

And now our lives are over
And now we kneel at the knees
    of Time
And now the henchman has
completed his task against a
backdrop like an empty mirror
And now all that's left is
mechanical wandering and
    brutal resign
And now the devious victor's laugh
And now the slow silence creeping
into our joints like the beetle's
    prowl

Worn thin from the inside out.
The soft protection, delicate,
is unraveling into the
strong fade.

No one, not even the tight
woven goddess hands of her,
could stop my disappearance now.
There is barely enough of me
left for even the hounds to smell.

I am going—
invisible as the breeze,
but weaker, much weaker—
unnoticed.

The vision too is mortal and
fleeting—dies long before we do.
And then, when it is gone
and we are fierce, we are
left to wander back to ourselves,
to our hollow caves,
to wait and mourn the brief trails
of color that carried us to
countries built upon one more lie.
No praise. No curses. No prayers.
We're ruined now and too perfect
    for that.

INVOLUNTARY SECRETS

Museums and libraries are the true churches, the real houses of God.

To search is to rebel against the foundations, social and moral codes, and cruel functions of society in order to transcend into a truer and more free nature. Art aids the search.

Art springs from an absence. Something doesn't exist in the world for the artist, something the artist needs to see or hear or otherwise experience, so the artist conjures the creation and brings it into being. Art fills a void.

Religion is the substratum of art. To wake to the mystery and rebuild God, to bring Him back down among us.

Since the world has been shattered long ago all that's left for the artist is to evaluate one's personal response to one's own splintered existence in relation to the splintered world.

Above all, Art should be interpretation. Upon experiencing a work the response should be *Yes! This helps me, I can use this. I see a little better now.*

Art is meant to help us, to heal. It allows both the artist and the audience to learn about themselves, and, subsequently, about the nature of life in general. It can help us see penetratingly deeper into existence. It is a necessity, an act of spiritual cultivation. Pursuit of self and spiritual cultivation is our highest duty.

God should be in every artistic endeavor.

The poet feasts on what others refuse to acknowledge, abandon.

The best way is to receive as much learning as possible—have a deep sense of education—but retain all primeval instincts and celebrate their natural splendor and mystery.

Beware of becoming too wise. Wisdom, though duly coveted aspiration, inhibits the will to action and discolors life.

Art is a race against death.

Companionship is not worth the concession of personality or values.

Love is the most capricious and illusionistic animal that has ever existed, so why does it persist? Why haven't we annihilated the beast centuries ago?

"I need you" is more accurate than "I love you". The illusion of love is developed out of a need, and it is the voids within that produce that need.

Courage and deep inner strength could conquer love.

Parents create memories for the child; orchestrate its mind, like staging a film in slow sculpted Time.

Life I love—life is ribbed wonder, splendor awe. It's man's invention of living that destroys me.

Enlightenment, or the path toward enlightenment, comes from the ceaseless act of asking questions, and the unending search for the answers to those questions.

There is no reward for what you discover on the search but the discovery itself.

More important than "reality" as you see it or are affected by it, more important than social commentary invoking change in social conditions, more important than political abrasion, first you must become spiritually aware—illuminated. Inner awareness is the root principle to all social change. First turn on to your god potential, then you may find the rest takes care of itself.

Those who always seek control, who want to take charge and dictate and order, are mistaken. If life is anything it is constant flux and disorder, elusive and ever-changing. Our lives should reflect that.

The lobotomy was a systematic imposition of order, control; subtle murder like television, or the workaday job.

Money has replaced the hunt.

We built the rules and attributed them to God. God became a super despotic Being with an omniscient hidden face. It's a metaphor for our own conscience. The rules are to help us live with ourselves; leave the word God out of it.

Do anything that satisfies. There are no rules except the ones you impose upon yourself. If you can live with yourself while pursuing your innocence you will never leave the Garden. The Christian conception of God and the symbol of Jesus have been manipulated by the Occidental world for centuries as one more way to control and oppress the masses; morality and guilt have been their tools.

Seek innocence!

Confronting death, not necessarily on a physical level, but simply contemplating death can restore spiritual life.

When I'm alone I feel as if I'm surrounded by spirits—and they're whispering.

Alliances, friendship, can be confining, a trap of prescribed role playing—mutant love game of power.

Time to kill the father all over again and run to freedom of the limitless self, anonymity.

Hidden and hiding, the life is not allowed to present itself outside the performance.

Now and then we must allow ourselves the luxury to grieve for ourselves.

We seek distraction from ourselves to escape what we cannot face—mortality's vacant eyes.

The flight from yourself is the flight toward yourself.

Only through recognition of the mystery and the power of the mystery will spiritual cultivation return.

www.ingramcontent.com/pod-product-compliance
Lightning Source LLC
Chambersburg PA
CBHW060318050426

42449CB00011B/2540